Effective Substitute Teachers

The Practicing Administrator's Leadership Series
Jerry J. Herman and Janice L. Herman, Editors

ROADMAPS
TO SUCCESS

Other Titles in This Series Include:

The Path to School Leadership: A Portable Mentor
Lee G. Bolman and Terrence E. Deal

Holistic Quality: Managing, Restructuring, and Empowering Schools
Jerry J. Herman

Selecting, Managing, and Marketing Technologies
Jamieson A. McKenzie

Individuals With Disabilities: Implementing the Newest Laws
Patricia F. First and Joan L. Curcio

Violence in the Schools: How to Proactively Prevent and Defuse It
Joan L. Curcio and Patricia F. First

Women in Administration: Facilitators for Change
L. Nan Restine

Power Learning in the Classroom
Jamieson A. McKenzie

Computers: Literacy and Learning
A Primer for Administrators
George E. Marsh II

Restructuring Schools: Doing It Right
Mike M. Milstein

Reporting Child Abuse:
A Guide to Mandatory Requirements for School Personnel
Karen L. Michaelis

Handbook on Gangs in Schools:
Strategies to Reduce Gang-Related Activities
Shirley R. Lal, Dhyan Lal, and Charles M. Achilles

Conflict Resolution: Building Bridges
Neil H. Katz and John W. Lawyer

Resolving Conflict Successfully: Needed Knowledge and Skills
Neil H. Katz and John W. Lawyer

Preventing and Managing Conflict in Schools
Neil H. Katz and John W. Lawyer

Secrets of Highly Effective Meetings
Maria M. Shelton and Laurie K. Bauer

(see back cover for additional titles)

Effective Substitute Teachers
Myth, Mayhem, or Magic?

Terrie St. Michel

CORWIN PRESS, INC.
A Sage Publications Company
Thousand Oaks, California

For information address:

Corwin Press, Inc.
A Sage Publications Company
2455 Teller Road
Thousand Oaks, California 91320

SAGE Publications Ltd.
6 Bonhill Street
London EC2A 4PU
United Kingdom

SAGE Publications India Pvt. Ltd.
M-32 Market
Greater Kailash I
New Delhi 110 048 India

Printed in the United States of America

Library of Congress Cataloging-in-Publication Data

St. Michel, Terrie.
    Effective substitute teachers : myth, mayhem, or magic? / Terrie
St. Michel
        p.   cm. — (Roadmaps to success)
    Includes bibliographical references.
    ISBN 0-8039-6248-7 (pbk.)
        1. Substitute teachers—United States.   I. Title.   II. Series.
LB2844.1.S8S9   1995
371.1′4111—dc20   95-1903

This book is printed on acid-free paper.

95 96 97 98 99 10 9 8 7 6 5 4 3 2 1

Corwin Press Production Editor: S. Marlene Head

Contents

Foreword

In far too many school districts, substitute teacher recruiting, training, and assistance are inefficient and ineffective. The result of this neglect of quality substitute services is that in classes where the substitute teacher is ill prepared or acting as a "baby-sitter," students don't learn.

Based on the results of her 2-year study of substitute teaching, Terrie St. Michel has produced an excellent and easily read book on the important topic of improving substitute teacher services to students. Her approach focuses on those responsible for ensuring the quality of substitute teaching: central office administrators, principals and assistant principals, regular classroom teachers, students, and substitute teachers themselves. Included are sample forms, examples, and a wide variety of helpful suggestions. In addition, an annotated bibliography is provided for those who wish to read further on this topic.

Whatever responsibility you share for ensuring the quality of substitute teaching—whether at the classroom, school, or district level—*Effective Substitute Teachers: Myth, Mayhem, or Magic?* will be your indispensible guidebook to improvement. If I were still a super-intendent of schools, I would buy a copy for every teacher and administrator in my school district.

JERRY J. HERMAN
JANICE L. HERMAN
Series Co-Editors

About the Author

Terrie St. Michel has been a member of the English department at South Mountain High School in Phoenix, Arizona—instructing students from all levels—for the past 13 years. She has also served as chair of this 50-member department and is presently the chair of the School Improvement Team (a site-based decision-making team). In addition to teaching, she also facilitates staff development offerings on her campus and throughout the Phoenix Union High School District. These professional activities range from writing across the curriculum to using computer software to improving the effectiveness of substitute teachers. Her background includes teaching physical education and social studies as well as English, and coaching a variety of sports. She received her bachelor's, master's, and doctoral degrees in education from Arizona State University.

During the past 5 years, St. Michel has presented workshops and inservices at various national conferences such as the National Council of Teachers of English, Association of Teacher Educators, National Council for the Social Studies, and Association for Supervision and Curriculum Development regarding substitute teacher programs, teaming, and issues related to school restructuring. Participants have ranged from elementary schools to colleges, and from administrators to regular teachers to college students to substitute teachers. She has published several articles on a variety of topics: leading schoolwide change, the benefits of using class journals, case studies, and issues involving substitute teachers. Her articles have appeared in *English Leadership Quarterly, SCOPE: Journal of the Arizona Association of Supervision and Curriculum Development,* and *Conference for Secondary School English Department Chairpersons Quarterly.* In addition, she has contributed case studies to *Staff Development Case Studies* (1992), edited by Judith H. Shulman and Amelia Mesa-Bains, and *Uncovering the Curriculum: Whole Language in Secondary and Post-Secondary Classrooms* (1993), authored by Kathleen and James Strickland. She has coauthored reference manuals for substitute teachers and regular teachers for the Phoenix Union High School District as well as a "how-to" manual for substitutes for the Association of Teacher Educators.

Introduction

They did nothing because they could only do a little.

—Carlos Cortez

A s a classroom teacher and department chair, I have grappled with how best to handle substitute teachers. Wouldn't it be great if every substitute teacher was competent and qualified to teach the subject he or she was assigned? And regular teachers always left detailed, easy-to-follow lesson plans that engaged students in meaningful activities? And there were enough keys to classrooms, the staff bathrooms, and lounges? And staff were extending and helpful, even if it was during their planning period? And the campus map was printed clearly and buildings were easy to find and readily accessible? And students were well-behaved, stayed on task without threats, and exhibited "good manners"? And substitutes left thorough notes describing how the day had gone, what had been accomplished, and what next needed to be done? And an administrator or department chair had stopped by during the course of the day to see how things were going and to offer feedback to the substitute? And students went home and told their parents how much they enjoyed the substitute teacher they'd had that day and how much they'd learned? And the regular teacher would return the following day to find everything the way it had been left, that the students knew the material they had covered, and the same substitute was requested for any future absences? Well, that may be how it is at Mt. Olympus Academy, but where I come from, this scenario is merely myth. In my experience, the situation is *very* different. Mayhem is the norm.

Ugh! What a mess! Administrators grumble about the uselessness of substitutes and trade horror stories:

"Last week I had to go into Room 39 six times to break up fights."

"Yesterday I was called to Room 8 because two students were fighting while the teacher was looking for another student who was missing!"

"Last year we had this one sub who was asking students out on dates!"

"The third grade classes went to the zoo last month, and one class had a substitute who didn't know how many kids were in the class because no attendance roster had been left. Luckily they must have all made it home okay because I haven't had any parents calling me looking for their child from that trip."

"The sub in photo lab 'borrowed' two cameras."

Teachers complain in faculty lounges:

"Why can't subs follow my lesson plans?"

"Yesterday my sub didn't show up for the first half of my first class."

"They didn't even get a sub for me!"

"The subs on this campus are the dregs of the earth!"

"Oh, no, I have to cover a class today."

Students yell to one another in hallways:

"Hey, we have a sub today!"

"Sub! Sub! Sub!"

"Oh, no, not another sub!"

In short, there are many who believe that substitutes are a menace. At best, they are considered necessary evils. A retired principal of 30 years succinctly summarized the situation: "The regular teacher is gone and the person we are putting in the room is a stranger who knows nothing." The result of this perception has been to hire substitutes merely to serve as glorified baby-sitters. Basically, they are expected to maintain control in the classroom, take roll, and come and go quietly and without incident. As for the students, a day spent with a substitute is too often a complete waste of time and too often a boring day in which students think of their own solutions to their boredom.

I have struggled with finding ways to improve the effectiveness of substitutes. After all, if student achievement is to increase, then instruction time must be maximized—*every* day. Therefore, I conducted a comprehensive, 2-year study to research the substitute teacher situation in order to establish who substitute teachers really are, what they actually do, and how effective they are from the perspectives of substitutes themselves, the students they serve, the regular teachers they replace, and the administrators who supervise them. The results of that study led to knowledge of how the current situation can be improved. The purpose of this book is to accomplish what most people think is impossible: to provide regular teachers and administrators with accurate information and specific recommendations for designing, implementing, and maintaining quality substitute teacher programs.

The issue of substitutes is extremely complex. The common response of the education system has been to ignore it and hope that nothing gets broken. As one principal put it, "Every morning I watch these substitutes walk into the office and I pray that each sub gets through the day without an incident." Another principal stands in the front office watching substitutes check in, thinking, "Will this one make it? Will that one be 'trouble'?" Like most, however, these fervent prayers and hopes are *all* that occurs to them to do to improve the situation.

The problems plaguing substitute teaching programs are more often the result of *nonmanagement* rather than mismanagement. I believe that we—administration, regular teachers, students, and substitutes—are all responsible for the existing problems and that together we can make positive changes that will make our students' lives richer. This is a situation where doing anything will result in a dramatic improvement—even magic!

Assessing the Need

Education is irrelevant to those without hope, and succeeds remarkably well for those who have it.

—David C. Berliner

There are numerous reasons why teachers spend time outside their classrooms: illness, family responsibilities, personal reasons, school business (e.g., professional conferences and meetings), and staff development programs. What is most important with regard to the common practice of using substitutes to replace regular teachers during absences is the effectiveness of those substitutes. Today, the demands for greater student achievement continue to increase, thereby raising the professional expectations of teachers. To meet these challenges, instruction time must be maximized, and those individuals who are asked to teach during the absence of the regular teachers must be equally effective in fulfilling the same roles.

Substitutes are expected to perform a variety of tasks as efficiently and effectively as the regular teachers whom they are replacing. Unfortunately, substitutes are usually ignored and too often given only minimal consideration by principals, regular teachers, and students. Yet substitutes are an invaluable resource and a vital component of the schooling process. Therefore, it is imperative that accurate descriptive data about substitute programs be collected and examined so that the policies and practices that involve substitutes can be addressed. A key issue is how substitutes are integrated into the school setting.

Describing the Typical Substitute Situation

Generally speaking, substitutes are a major force in today's schools. Unfortunately, research tells us that they receive very little support, no specialized training, and are rarely evaluated. The following describes a typical day (and may easily be a "best-case scenario") in the life of a substitute:

Once the decision has been made as to which campus a substitute will be assigned and for which classes, that substitute will probably have less than 1 hour in which to get ready and travel to the school site. The substitute will be expected to arrive on the campus at the same time as the regular teachers—regardless of the lead time he or she has been given.

Upon arriving at the campus, the substitute's first challenge will be to find a parking place, and then locate the administration building and the person in charge of providing necessary materials to substitutes. These materials will probably include a map of the campus and a bell schedule indicating when classes begin and end, lunch periods, and how much time is allowed between class periods. Keys to classrooms, restrooms, and staff lounges may also be given out by the principal's secretary or the security office.

Most of the time, the substitute will find that adequate lesson plans have been prepared (although an experienced substitute will also have his or her own backup set of plans). Only about half of the time can the substitute expect to find a group of students who have been notified in advance that they will be having a substitute teacher and what is expected of them during their regular teacher's absence.

Rarely will the substitute be evaluated or even asked how things are going by other staff. In short, the substitute will be expected to show up to each class on time, maintain order, take roll, carry out the lesson, and leave a note for the regular teacher about the classes and events of the day without support, encouragement, or acknowledgment.

The perception of students and teachers is that very little learning takes place when a substitute teaches; therefore, if prior planning for the substitute has occurred, the kinds of assignments the substitute undoubtedly will be asked to deliver will be worksheets or showing a film, or students will be expected to work independently. Any interaction between the substitute and students (aside from taking roll) will usually require initiation by the substitute. Engaging students in discussions can be a positive and rather simplistic way of establishing rapport.

Rarely will the substitute find up-to-date seating charts. Roll is usually taken by calling out students' names from an attendance roster or by passing around a sign-in sheet. The substitute will be at the mercy of the students who choose to cooperate because few teachers make a point of selecting reliable students who can assist the substitute.

The substitute will have no reference materials provided by the district, but will be expected to abide by the policies for proper conduct and follow the appropriate procedures for carrying out the many tasks expected of him or her. If a problem should arise, and help is requested, then the substitute can expect to be evaluated and possibly not asked back to that campus, regardless of the "problem."

At the end of the school day, the substitute will return to the principal's office to check out. After keys and any materials have been returned, the substitute may be thanked and allowed to leave.

The working conditions of substitutes are demanding—unfamiliar settings, new students, assignments out of their area of expertise, and frequently inadequate lesson plans. The daily rate of pay for substitutes is low and there are rarely any benefits offered. Too often their efforts are unrewarded and unappreciated. Amid these difficulties, many substitutes persist because they want full-time teaching positions and they want to be involved in teaching—in working with kids.

Using Questionnaires and Observations
to Identify Needs

Making quality decisions requires knowledge, experience, and accurate, up-to-date information. As educators, our responsibilities for providing quality education to all students continue to broaden and become more complex. All facets of the schooling process—from providing transportation and lunches to offering a rich curriculum and employing quality professionals—must be carefully examined and evaluated on an ongoing basis.

In assessing your substitute teacher program, you can use any one of the following questionnaires and observations in isolation, by mixing and matching, or as a comprehensive resource to measure your program. The questionnaires can be used on individual campuses or for all schools in the district. Because substitutes are hired and used in a variety of ways, it is recommended that you review all the suggested materials and then select the approach that best fits your needs and situation. The bottom line is that the more information you gather, the better equipped you will be for making those decisions involving the use of substitutes that will improve students' education.

There are five groups that should be contacted in order to attain the necessary data for analyzing your substitute program: the district director of personnel (assuming this is the individual who reviews the applications and conducts the initial interviews of all substitutes), principals on each campus, regular teachers, students (a representative sample can be used for this group), and the district's substitute teachers. Questionnaires can be used to gather data from each group. Attention should be given to designing questionnaire items so that continuity, focus, and purpose will remain consistent among them as well as provide additional relevant information specific to each group.

District Director of Personnel Questionnaire

The information gathered from the district director of personnel should focus on determining the policies, practices, and procedures for using substitutes. Specifically, the questionnaire should be designed to elicit information regarding the following:

Statistical Composition. How many students are in the district? How many teachers are in the district?

Employment Practices. Are substitute teachers in the district required to have the same minimum academic degree as regular teachers? Does the district give its substitutes any kind of special consideration if they apply for a regular teaching job?

Administrative Arrangements. Who is responsible for securing substitutes? Describe the procedure used to remove a substitute with poor performance records.

Resources. Does the district provide orientation programs for its substitutes? List the materials that the district provides to its substitutes.

Principal Questionnaire

The questionnaire completed by the principal should determine how well a campus's substitute teacher program works as well as point out those areas in which it can be improved. The questionnaire should elicit specific information about the interviewing practices of substitutes at the campus level. First, are substitutes interviewed? Interviews of substitutes should be conducted by the principal or a designee in order to ascertain the following:

Personal Attributes. Before choosing substitutes for your school, do you or your designee interview them first to assess their ability to adapt to new situations?

Professional Expertise. Before choosing substitutes for your school, do you first interview them to ascertain their area(s) of expertise?

Second, the principal's questionnaire should address questions that

Inquire About the Kinds of Information a Substitute Might Receive. Do substitutes receive campus procedures, campus map, bell schedules, lesson plans, needed resources, evaluation forms, and so on?

Identify Who is Responsible for Contacting and Recruiting Substitutes.
_____ is responsible for substitutes on our campus.

Describe the Evaluation Practices of Substitutes. Does one or more persons—a principal, assistant principal, staff development specialist, department chair, lead teacher—visit a substitute for a few minutes at least once during the day to evaluate the substitute's teaching ability?

Determine Whether There Is Some Form of Communication Between the Substitute and the Regular Teacher. Are substitutes given a form to complete at the end of the day so that regular teachers will know how the day went and what activities were started and/or completed?

Examine the End of the Day Follow-Up With Substitutes. Do you or your designee make a point of meeting with substitutes at the end of the school day to discuss how their day went?

Regular Teacher Questionnaire

Regular teachers should be asked questions regarding four broad areas:

Their Preparation for Substitutes. Do you leave lesson plans for substitutes?

Their Perceptions of Substitutes' Effectiveness in Delivering Instruction. Do you believe worthwhile instruction takes place in your absence?

Their Methods for Addressing Issues Concerning Discipline During Their Absence. What instructions do you leave for a substitute in terms of how to handle discipline problems?

General Information About Their Experiences With Substitutes. Do substitutes report that they had a positive experience with your classes?

Student Questionnaire

It is helpful to use a representative student sample to elicit feedback from students regarding their general experiences with substitutes. Questions should be designed to determine

Attitudes Students Have About Substitutes. Do you believe substitutes are as effective as your regular teachers?

Behaviors Exhibited by Students and Their Classmates During the Absence of the Regular Teacher. Are you cooperative when a substitute is teaching?

Activities in Which Students are Engaged. Are the kinds of assignments you are given when a substitute teaches usually handouts or worksheets?

Preparation of the Students for a Substitute. Do your teachers tell you in advance when you will have a substitute?

Students' Evaluation of Substitutes. Do your teachers ask for your reactions or comments about your substitute?

Students' Beliefs About Learning With a Substitute. Do you learn as much when a substitute is teaching a class as when your regular teacher is there?

Demographic Status of Students. I am in Grade __.

Attitudinal Information Regarding the Relationship Between Actions and Needs, Desires, Preferences, Motives, and Goals. What are your suggestions for substitute teachers?

Students' Experiences With Substitutes. Describe an experience you had this year with a substitute.

Substitute Teacher Questionnaire

Substitutes should be asked questions regarding their personal and professional characteristics.

Personal Background. What is your age? How long has it been since you earned your last degree? When you are not substituting, what are you doing?

Professional Roles. When a teacher has not left you lesson plans, do you have your own set of plans?

Expectations. Were expectations for substituting clearly explained to you? Did you receive any materials that explained what was required of substitutes?

Successes. When you are a substitute, how much do students learn? Describe how you know that you are successful.

Abilities and Professional Training. Have you ever received any in-service or training for substitute teaching? What particular abilities do you have that enable you to be an effective teacher?

Working Conditions. Did the regular teacher prepare adequate lesson plans for your use? What are the disadvantages of being a substitute?

Career Choice Reasons. Why are you a substitute?

Perceptions. In general, how would you describe the teachers in the schools where you have substituted? How do students perceive substitutes?

Routines. How many days a week do you usually substitute? Do you try to establish a relationship with a new class? If so, how do you accomplish this?

Substituting Experiences. How many days did you substitute last year? Describe the best conditions under which you have substituted. Explain why these conditions were the best.

Handling Discipline. Describe how you handle discipline problems—including any kind of preparation you do prior to meeting the class as well as what you do when confronted with unexpected problems.

Observations

Observations can be conducted to strengthen the validity of the findings generated from the questionnaires. The specific intent of these observations should be to document those routine and unpredictable events that occur in classrooms. A substitute observation report form can be designed to enhance the consistency with which the activities are recorded and to provide a structure for identifying the following elements of every observation: class period; subject; length of observation; date; school; segment of class period observed—beginning, middle, and/or end; specific information about the substitute (e.g., appearance, demeanor, area of expertise, etc.); students' behaviors; substitute's behaviors; and additional relevant information (e.g., directions on the chalkboard, handouts, interruptions, etc.).

Walking into classrooms where substitutes are teaching is very powerful. Regardless of the purpose, the effects are many: students' behaviors change, substitutes feel validated, and the observer gains firsthand knowledge of what's really going on. In just a few short minutes (10 usually suffices), an observer (who could be the principal, an assistant principal, a department chair, a staff development specialist, or any designated teacher) can determine the extent to which the class was prepared for the substitute, the kinds of activities provided, the degree of rapport, and the overall effectiveness of the substitute in handling a classroom of students. Observations are clearly the most immediately and comprehensively effective means for determining what substitutes are actually doing.

Substitutes, Student Achievement, and Wasted Resources

One of the primary concerns of all educators is student achievement. Keeping students on task and learning is one of our greatest challenges—it is at the heart of what we do. But regular teachers often report that they are frustrated when they return from an absence because the substitute either did not cover the materials left, chose to use his or her own lesson, or simply allowed the students to do nothing. Regular teachers complain about having to reteach material covered by the substitute and needing to spend extra time reviewing when lessons were ignored during their absence. The more days the regular teacher is absent, the greater the potential for wasted learning time.

Part of the confusion for substitutes is the result of being assigned to areas in which they are inexperienced and unfamiliar with the content or grade level of students. In addition, substitutes are rarely given advance notice of their assignments, which makes it difficult for them to review the regular teacher's lesson plans and to prepare for the students. There are also those times when adequate lesson plans have not been left.

Unfortunately, a day spent with a substitute teacher is often a day off. When taking into consideration that substitutes are filling in for regular teachers a conservatively estimated average of 10 days per year, then it is clear that an enormous amount of instructional time is being unnecessarily wasted.

To better understand the magnitude of the instructional time carried out by substitutes, it is helpful to examine the statistics collected from a large urban high school district of 15 campuses serving 19,500 students and employing 1,200 regular teachers and 500 substitute teachers. During a 7-year period (1986-1993), the average number of days regular teachers were absent because of *school business* was 4,303. When this figure is multiplied by five (the average number of class periods a regular teacher is assigned each day), the number of class periods filled in by substitutes was 21,515. When other reasons for absences by regular teachers were considered (e.g., illness, family responsibilities, or personal reasons), the number of days that a substitute was teaching in place of the regular teacher was tripled! For example, in 1992-1993, the total number of absences for regular teachers equaled 14,229 days. Multiplying this figure by five resulted in a whopping 71,145 class periods that were taught by substitutes during the 1992-1993 school year!

What is even more disconcerting about these statistics is that the hidden absences and resulting class coverage that are a part of most schools are not reflected in these figures. For example, on days when there are not enough substitutes and regular teachers are asked to cover a colleague's class during his or her preparation period for additional salary (e.g., $15 per class covered), a substitute is not hired and the teacher absence is often not properly recorded. There are also incidents of colleagues privately agreeing to cover one another's classes. Many times there are unexpected events that occur that require regular teachers to miss one or more class periods (e.g., a parent shows up on campus and demands a conference or a teacher's expertise is needed to resolve some crisis) and "someone" is sent to "watch the students" until the regular teacher can return.

All of this adds up to enormous amounts of lost instructional time. If the person replacing the regular teacher is not an experienced and qualified professional, and the regular teacher has not prepared adequately for his or her absence, then the instructional time is wasted. It is possible that inadequate coverage may even create a situation of reducing meaningful time on task in the future because of the regular teacher's need to reteach or conduct additional reviews of previously covered materials.

As for the financial costs of allowing valuable instructional time to be squandered, the sum can be staggering. Using the same school district mentioned earlier (which pays its substitutes $50 per day, and $15 per class period to regular teachers who are enlisted to fill in for colleagues), on a typical day an average of 140 substitutes is used. This equates to $7,000 per day in additional teaching salaries. In 1992-1993, when the number of regular teacher absences was 14,229, a total of $711,450 was paid to substitutes. This figure does not include any of the regular teacher payouts of $15 per class period, which can add up quickly.

For example, on the campus where I teach, an estimated 30 to 50 class periods per day are covered "in-house" at a cost of $450 to $750 per day and $80,100 to $111,250 per school year for one campus! This expense could be reduced by hiring an additional 10 substitutes at $50 per day each or $89,000 per school year. The money for these additional 10 substitutes would be well spent in that this constant pool of available substitutes would create less disruption and provide more continuity.

Finally, more attention must be paid to matching substitutes' assignments with their areas of expertise. When substitutes are experienced and knowledgeable, they have a much better chance of accurately carrying out the regular teachers' lesson plans and engaging the students in meaningful learning activities for the duration of the class period or school day.

When substitutes are given little support, direction, and acknowledgment, then everyone's resources are squandered. In this day and age, when rising absenteeism and poor academic performance are on the increase, as educators we cannot afford to waste even a single class period. We must seize the moment, plan ahead, and carry out our obligations as a unified professional team.

Summary

Substitute teaching is a difficult and demanding job with few rewards. In order to improve the effectiveness of substitutes in carrying out their many tasks, the current state of a substitute program must be determined. Questionnaires and observations can be used to collect the necessary baseline data.

The kinds of information gathered from the questionnaires should focus on statistical data, employment procedures, resources, management practices, attitudinal perspectives, exhibited behaviors, shared beliefs, expectations and methods of evaluation. Observations of substitutes should be conducted to assess what is actually taking place in classrooms as well as to help set the tone that substitutes are to be teaching and that learning is to be taking place, not mere baby-sitting.

Valuable instructional time that is too often lost when a substitute teaches can be recovered and the use of resources maximized by improving the hiring, managing, and evaluating practices of our substitute programs.

Defining the Players
and Their Roles

You cannot effectively lead someone somewhere unless you have been there yourself.

—G. Lynn Nelson

The effectiveness of substitute teachers is a reflection of the effort invested by all stakeholders involved—administrators, regular teachers, students, and finally, substitutes themselves. If any one of these groups fails to fulfill its obligations, then the degree to which substitutes can successfully fill in for regular teachers is significantly reduced.

Substitutes and Expectations

The stereotypical views commonly held about substitutes are that (a) they cannot get regular teaching jobs because their skills are inadequate or (b) they are mothers who are using substitute teaching as a means of supplementing their income while they raise their children, thus making them ideal baby-sitters. Who substitutes really are, is a mystery to administrators and regular teachers. There is much ambiguity about the role that substitutes are to play in the schooling process, a fact which further complicates the abilities of substitutes to carry out their responsibilities. Compounding this confusion about substitutes' roles is the uncertainty about what administrators should be doing in relation to improving the use of substitutes and how regular teachers can be more responsible in planning for their absences by providing the necessary materials and preparing their students.

Effective substitutes are the result of every person doing his or her part. Although there are always exceptions, the majority of substitutes can be more effective in delivering worthwhile instruction, and the overall substitute program can be dramatically improved. For these reasons, an accurate description of who the "players" are and their roles is needed.

Many substitutes have several years of experience working with children and are well educated. They are not simply "warm bodies off the street," but rather are caring, dedicated, and hardworking professionals. According to the research about substitutes, it is reasonable to assume that a pool of substitutes will very likely be composed of an equal number of males and females of varying ages. A large portion of the substitutes will be made up of individuals who are seeking permanent teaching jobs. Other common reasons for choosing to substitute include wanting to have a job that offers considerable flexibility, a desire to work with children, fewer responsibilities than a full-time position, and supplementing a retirement income. Unfortunately, substitutes are seldom evaluated and rarely conferenced about their performance, so it is difficult to assess their classroom skills.

Although substitutes experience little acknowledgment for their efforts and are not perceived as part of the education setting, they report that they enjoy their work. In addition, they are receptive to participating in training that may help them improve their skills. Substitutes are committed to carrying out their tasks in a professional manner and contributing something of value to the students with whom they interact. In short, they are ready, willing, and able no matter what the expectation.

The ideal substitute teacher is a professional who follows school policies and procedures and has the ability to carry out a variety of teaching assignments. A strong desire to work with students and a positive attitude toward evaluation and suggestions for improvement are also desirable characteristics for substitutes. Additionally, in terms of teaching skills, the ideal substitute teacher is able to motivate students by recognizing their diversity and allowing them to work independently or in groups. First-rate substitutes know the subject matter and are able to use a variety of instructional techniques to stimulate creative and original thought as well as to reinforce positive student behavior. Finally, the personal characteristics of a superior substitute suggest someone who is enthusiastic and understanding, respectful and patient, friendly and positive, dependable and punctual, confident and competent. Ultimately, substitute teachers want the same kind of authority, privileges, and responsibilities extended to regular teachers. They are professionals who want to be treated as such.

Who substitute teachers are depends to some extent on who we perceive them to be and how we treat them. There is much agreement that substitutes are necessary for carrying out the daily operations of schools. Yet there is little interest paid to substitutes in way of evaluation and follow-up to determine what they are actually doing with the students. Rarely does an administrator interact with substitutes, unless, of course, the substitute has a problem. Regular teachers do not go out of their way to work with or interact with substitutes aside from requesting that substitutes leave written notes about their experiences. Even though teachers want substitutes to be well prepared, informed, and ready to teach, they still regard them as mere "placeholders" who mark time until the regular teacher returns. This is especially evident in the kinds of assignments teachers leave for students—they seldom require anything more of the substitute than to pass out worksheets or turn on a videotape.

The most hostile pictures of substitutes come from students who resent their regular teachers' absences. Students feel that if there is so much emphasis placed on their daily attendance, then why shouldn't their teachers have to be there too? In contrast with their feelings of abandonment, students also understand how difficult it is to be a substitute and expect their regular teachers to inform them about anticipated absences and to hold them accountable for behaving appropriately. Students perceive substitutes to be just that—substitutes.

Substitute teachers are expected to do it all. Principals expect substitutes to fill in for the regular teachers who are absent by carrying out various job responsibilities that include taking attendance, following the prescribed lesson plans, and maintaining order. Regular teachers expect substitutes to follow the lesson plans left for them, maintain the physical integrity of the classroom, maintain control of the students, and communicate with them about their substitute experience. Students expect substitutes to know the subject matter and engage them in meaningful instructional activities.

Aside from what substitutes are expected to do, there is the issue of what they actually accomplish. Unlike the misconceptions held about substitutes, most substitutes are, in fact, competent in taking attendance, following the regular teacher's lesson plans, and maintaining the classroom (from both a physical perspective and with regard to handling disruptions).

Given the difficulty in understanding all that substitutes do, it would be to their advantage if they recorded the dates, schools, courses, grade levels, teachers, and any comments they may have in some type of personal log. They should also spend a few minutes at the end of each day reviewing their performance: what went well, what could be improved, what they enjoyed most, and what nonteaching duties they may have performed.

This kind of self-evaluation log can be used when applying for permanent teaching positions to show prospective employers their work history record and that they take initiative and are self-reflective. This log will also help them improve their skills and enable them to recognize areas in which they have difficulties. This kind of personal feedback can also help provide a sense of satisfaction to these individuals, who receive very few thanks for their efforts.

In short, substitutes are expected to carry out the same responsibilities as regular teachers. Given the lack of support and consideration shown to them, they succeed remarkably well.

Administrators

District personnel in charge of hiring, assigning, and retaining substitutes must set high standards. Absence records that indicate patterns of behavior (e.g., How many substitutes are requested during the school year?) as well as general areas of need (e.g., Which day of the week do we use the most substitutes?) should be kept. This information can help principals predict when they will need the most substitutes and enable them to make arrangements in advance for substitute coverage. Districts should also provide preservice workshops for substitutes prior to the beginning of the school year and then offer follow-up staff development programs throughout the year.

Perhaps the most significant steps that districts can take to improve their substitute teacher programs are to offer competitive salaries, fringe benefits (e.g., health insurance), and opportunities to be hired full-time or placed on a "preferred substitute list." These kinds of incentives will attract the best substitutes and ensure a reliable pool from which to draw at all times. A good question to ask is, "What are we offering that is better and different from other school districts?"

The hiring of quality substitutes is another important role carried out by administration. The same careful consideration used when hiring regular teachers should also be given when hiring substitutes. Although it is difficult to determine an individual's future behavior in the classroom setting, when conducting interviews, administrators should consider (a) the flexibility of the candidate, (b) the ability of the candidate to adapt to various classroom settings (e.g., gymnasiums to self-contained classrooms to chemistry labs to learning centers), (c) whether or not the candidate will be able to establish rapport with all types of student groups and create a positive classroom environment for learning, (d) the variety of subject fields in which he or she is knowledgeable and capable of teaching, and (e) whether or not the candidate is a likable person who will get along with others.

Administration must also establish parameters for holding regular teachers accountable for such things as (a) up-to-date seating charts and attendance rosters; (b) lesson plans that extend the curriculum and provide for active participation—lessons that are not merely "busy work"; (c) preparing their students for a substitute prior to being absent, including discussing their expectations for students' behavior and briefly describing the kinds of activities in which students will be involved; (d) identifying at least two reliable students per class who can be counted on to assist the substitute; (e) following up once they have returned by asking students about their experiences with the substitute and recording both students' and their own comments on a feedback form to be filed; (f) following all proper procedures for requesting a substitute; and (g) communicating with colleagues about their absence and lesson plans in case the substitute has any difficulties.

Soliciting feedback from students about their substitute experiences is also important. Principals should make a point of interacting with students to stay in touch with the pulse of the campus; this is an ideal opportunity to inquire about substitutes. After all, informal conversations can be very revealing. What is important is including the students and giving them an opportunity to share their experiences and suggestions.

Parents may be another group from whom principals will want to ask for feedback regarding substitutes. Principals may want to ask parents to report to the office any complaints or comments their children may make about substitutes. Questions and discussions about substitutes can be initiated at parent meetings, through newsletters, or during conferences. Parents are concerned about their children's education and want to be reassured that worthwhile activities are taking place every day. They may even be interested in becoming substitutes themselves, and application information should be given to them.

Principals, assistant principals, department chairs, staff development specialists, and lead teachers should be encouraged to routinely go into classrooms and observe substitutes in action. A standardized substitute evaluation form may help increase the observation practices of substitutes and establish reliable performance records for future reference. Using a standardized form may also help involve regular teachers in improving the use of substitutes by establishing a routine for accountability. In turn, substitutes should also be given a form for reporting their experiences (see Resource A). The substitute evaluation form should include (a) the date of evaluation; (b) the names of the school, the substitute, the absent teacher, and the evaluator; (c) the substitute's area of expertise; (d) comments on personal characteristics—attitude, interactions with staff and students, punctuality, and so on; (e) comments on teaching characteristics—knowledge of content, instructional delivery, ability to follow lesson plans, classroom management, and so on; (f) the quality of substitute feedback left for the regular teacher; (g) whether or not the substitute was teaching in his or her area of expertise; (h) a place where recommendation for continued reemployment at that campus can be noted; (i) an area for general comments; and (j) a place for the signatures of both the evaluator and the substitute.

Regular Teachers and Students

Ideally, substitutes should replace regular teachers with as little break in routine as possible. Regular teachers should be expected to plan materials for the substitute as well as prepare their students. During emergencies or when teachers are unexpectedly absent, it may not be possible to inform their students, but emergency lesson plans should nevertheless be on file and available to substitutes. Additionally, up-to-date seating charts will enable the substitute to take roll efficiently and call on students during class discussions. As a part of the classroom routine, reliable students who can assist the substitute should be identified. Lesson plans must be concise and readable and must incorporate both individual and group activities.

Prior to needing a substitute, the regular teacher should work with his or her students to establish cooperative behaviors. When students are included in the planning process, given specific directions as to expected behavior, and given opportunities to evaluate the substitute, then there is the potential for them to feel empowered and to respond more responsibly when the regular teacher is absent. Students are a crucial component to the success of any substitute, and regular teachers must remember that students are the consumers who interact directly with substitutes. Therefore, soliciting student cooperation is an important key to the effectiveness of the substitute.

When students are asked to respond in writing (rather than merely verbalizing in a less structured fashion), a sense of importance about their perceptions and experiences is created. Information about any particular substitute teacher can be kept on file, and the regular teacher can use the students' feedback to improve his or her plans for future absences. Students can be asked questions such as (a) How did the class period go? (b) In what way(s) did you contribute to making the classroom a positive experience? (c) How would you describe the behavior of your classmates? and (d) What can I do in the future to improve your substitute experience? The key is to make students feel that they have a voice in how they are treated and to help them understand that they can make a difference.

It is helpful to keep in mind how students feel when their regular teachers are absent—they resent it. With so much emphasis placed on them to show up for classes every day, they feel their teachers ought to provide the example and be there every day, too. When their regular teachers are not there, students want to be engaged in worthwhile activities that have been clearly explained to them and their substitutes. Students also want to know in advance when they are going to have a substitute. Ideally, students would prefer to have the same substitute so that they can get to know him or her and so that the substitute can get to know them and their normal routines. Education is about relationships between staff and students, and this extends to substitutes as well.

Students hold the regular teachers accountable for the quality of their experiences when substitutes are teaching. They expect their teachers to leave clear and organized instructions so that the substitute will know what to do and be able to conduct worthwhile lessons. Students also want cooperation and to be held accountable for acting responsibly when their regular teacher is absent. Additionally, they expect their regular teachers to discipline those students who are disruptive and uncooperative. Finally, students want to be asked for feedback about their substitute experience. They need an opportunity to share concerns and frustrations that might not otherwise be addressed.

When regular teachers are remiss in holding themselves and their students accountable, then students follow their lead; this is when they cause disruptions and are uncooperative. It is their way of saying, "Our teacher doesn't care what we do, so why should we?" Students want structure and quality interaction—they are in school to learn. They expect and want substitutes to take charge of the class and to teach them rather than merely baby-sit them. They recognize that their behavior can make their substitute experience a positive one or simply a waste of time. Students look to their regular teachers to set standards, provide a framework, and enforce consequences. Students will respond when informed and held accountable—students will fulfill our expectations.

Students' expectations of substitutes are the most demanding, as well as the most consistent with the kinds of expectations we all have for our substitutes. Specifically, students want substitutes to teach, know the content, and maintain order. Although most students perceive substitutes to be just that—substitutes—they also understand the difficulties and feel that their regular teachers should be responsible for setting the tone and holding them accountable. In fact, student disruptions are the exception, not the rule, and those classrooms that operate successfully and productively on a daily basis fare much better when a substitute is teaching than those where even the regular teacher has problems.

Students' behaviors are fairly consistent from one day to the next—when the expectations are high normally, then students can be expected to maintain the same high standards when the regular teacher is absent. When asked what regular teachers could do to improve students' substitute experience, one student suggested that the regular teacher should "have a talk with the students about substitutes and tell them that they should respect the substitutes and thank them for coming and substituting." Another student was direct and to the point, "Teach students to be more respectful."

In order for substitutes to fulfill the many roles expected of them, everyone—from the principal to the students—must contribute. Substituting is probably the most difficult and demanding job within the field of education and the one that receives the least amount of attention and support. Positive changes in our substitute programs will require a true team effort.

Summary

Substitutes are diverse, trained individuals who enjoy working with kids. Many are pursuing a permanent teaching position or using substituting as a means of supplementing their income.

Administrators must provide a supportive framework for substitutes and ensure that all stakeholders are fulfilling their obligations. They are responsible for conducting evaluations and holding regular teachers accountable when they are absent.

Regular teachers must follow the proper procedures for securing substitutes and then prepare meaningful lessons. They must take into account emergency situations and describe any nonteaching duties that their substitutes may be expected to carry out. They should also inform their students of their absence and specify how their students should behave.

Students will fulfill our expectations; they can be either helpful or disruptive. Therefore, lessons should be meaningful and directions for completing assignments should be clear and easy to follow. Upon their return, the regular teachers should ask students about their substitute experience and hold them accountable for turning in all assigned work.

Effective substitutes reflect the degree to which all stakeholders have done their part.

Read the Manual!

There is one thing stronger than all the armies of the world and that is an idea whose time has come.

—Victor Hugo

Increasing the effectiveness of substitute teachers also requires providing them with information about the district, instructional strategies, evaluation procedures, and tips for success. Reference manuals for substitutes should include information on these five areas:

1. An overview of the general expectations and conduct policies of the district
2. Specific information regarding the central office and all the campuses
3. Various feedback forms that substitutes are expected to use as well as the evaluation form that will be used in assessing their performance
4. Suggestions and strategies for substitutes to use in the classroom as they interact with students

5. Generic lessons, outlines for creating lessons, and helpful hints for how to be prepared at all times for all occasions

Regular teachers also need a reference manual to help them better plan and prepare for their substitutes. Regular teachers (although absent) are still responsible for their students in terms of behavior and instruction; therefore, reference manuals for regular teachers should address these four areas:

1. An overview of the purpose of such a manual and how it fits into the overall scheme of their professional duties
2. Managerial considerations essential for ensuring successful substitute coverage
3. Arranging for substitute coverage whether the need be predetermined or arise unexpectedly
4. Evaluating the substitute experience

Knowing what to do and how to do it is essential for both substitutes and regular teachers. After all, the goal is to have a smooth transition from the time substitutes are notified of their assignments to their carrying out the regular teachers' lessons and, finally, to the end-of-the-day checkout.

Information, Strategies, Policies, and Tips

In many respects, substitute teachers should be given the same kinds of information as regular teachers; after all, they are legally just as accountable for the students with whom they interact as regular teachers. From the district's perspective, substitutes should be given such information as a job description (this can be adapted from that of the regular teacher's job description); expectations about their assignments (e.g., where to report; how they will be notified and by whom; whether or not it is okay to refuse an assignment or to request certain content areas, certain campuses, and/or days of the week, etc.); district policies (e.g., standards of employee conduct, salary, child abuse issues, contract obligations, and inadequate service procedures, etc.); and central office information (e.g., names of people in charge of hiring and assigning substitutes, principals and their secretaries, etc.).

In addition to this information regarding the district as a whole, substitutes should also be given specific information about each school: names of schools, contact person(s) and their telephone numbers, check-in location, nonteaching duties, campus map (with check-in location and parking areas clearly marked) and bell schedules, special events calendar, and fire drill procedures with evacuation map.

Aside from this basic list of district and campus information, substitutes should also be provided with information regarding evaluation policies and procedures, classroom management strategies, techniques for better instruction, and tips for professional success.

Regular teachers need to know what to do to prepare for their substitutes, how to arrange for coverage for both planned and unexpected absences, and how evaluations of their substitutes will be conducted. Many of the same suggestions provided for substitutes can be shared with the regular teachers. Schools or districts may want to create some kind of double-sided "quick reference" sheet for use by regular teachers and substitutes that lists those essentials for survival: location of the staff restrooms, the substitute service telephone number, what to do if the classroom key does not work, what to do if a student walks out of the classroom, who to contact in case of an emergency, and so on.

User-Friendly Reference Manuals for Substitutes

Developing user-friendly reference manuals for substitute teachers requires merely gathering the necessary information, organizing it, and compiling it into spiral or three-ring notebooks. The advantages to using three-ring notebooks are that updated and additional materials can be added to them at any time and substitutes will have a place to keep their notes and other paperwork. This notebook can be divided into five sections: overview, district and campus information, evaluations and feedback, classroom management, and lessons.

The introductory overview section should include a letter to the substitutes welcoming them to the district and describing the purpose of the reference manual. A rationale for the manual, explaining the important role that substitutes fill within the district and the expectations for instructional continuity when regular teachers are absent, may also be included. Specifically, the district may want to emphasize that there is an expectation that worthwhile lessons will take place during the absence of the regular teachers and that both substitutes and regular teachers will be held accountable for meaningful student activity.

Presenting substitutes with objectives can also be included in the overview section and may help provide focus. An objective may read, "This substitute reference manual provides instructional materials to substitutes that emphasize critical thinking skills through reading, writing, listening, and discussing."

Professional tips can also be included in this opening section. The following are suggested tips:

1. Follow the lesson plans provided by the regular teacher.
2. Interact with the students by walking around the classroom, asking questions, and engaging students in discussions about the lesson.
3. Be prepared with your own set of generic lesson plans for unexpected emergencies and to fill in gaps in the regular teacher's plans.
4. Always leave detailed notes about the students (including those who were helpful), what was accomplished, what needs to be done next, and the general tone of the class.

Although few school districts have job descriptions written especially for substitutes, some kind of job description should be provided. The purpose of a job description is to serve as a guide that states the general responsibilities and major duties of those hired to fill the position. A job description for substitutes may include these items:

1. Provide appropriate classroom instruction for subject and grade level taught.

2. Be responsible for timely, neat, accurate, and complete records and their submission.
3. Check in and out each day with the designated campus personnel.
4. Leave detailed notes for the regular teacher about how the day went.
5. Carry out other duties (e.g., monitoring playgrounds and lunch areas) as indicated by the principal (or designee).

Finally, the overview should conclude with the district's policies that govern substitutes (e.g., general considerations, major areas of conduct, staff-student relations, etc.).

The second section, district and campus information, should contain a school calendar; the district office address, telephone numbers of key personnel, and office hours; the names of each principal, school, and secretary, and their telephone numbers; and specific information about each campus (e.g., who to report to for check-in and where that person is located, where to secure keys, various campus procedures, nonteaching duties, etc.), including maps and bell schedules.

The evaluations and feedback section should present an overview of the evaluation process and the guidelines it follows. Samples of all evaluation and feedback forms should be included so that administrators, regular teachers, and substitutes know exactly what will be reviewed and recorded.

The classroom management section is a broad area that can be used to offer helpful hints to substitutes on how to interact with students in positive ways so that learning can take place during the absence of the regular teachers. Policies concerning discipline practices should be described; perhaps a copy of the referral form to be used should be included. However, a word of caution—classroom management that focuses on the negative may result in an emphasis on discipline rather than instruction. A statement that referrals are a last resort and that planning and meaningful activities are the keys to cooperation in the classroom should precede the discussion on how to handle "problems." Substitutes should be encouraged to catch students doing something right and keep them on task in order to minimize disruptions.

A few firsthand vignettes by substitutes about their experiences may be included to provide insights about the daily routine of substitutes. Sometimes it helps to know that others have had similar experiences. For example, one substitute described the worst conditions in which he had substituted: "My worst experience was the first time I subbed. I went into a classroom and I had a film to show. Plus, I let the kids walk all over me. Some of them read. I was very nervous."

The final section, lessons, should include a discussion about the key components of structuring lessons (e.g., objectives, student activities, important terms, and concluding activities) and delivering instruction (e.g., planning to use the entire class period, being familiar with the lesson, and ensuring that all necessary supplies are available). Examples of lesson plan formats should be included to help substitutes who may have to create their own.

Generic lesson plans for each subject offered (e.g., English, math, physical education, foreign language, third grade, kindergarten, etc.) are an important inclusion for this section. Generic lessons should be designed in such a way that the substitute will have student activities that cover the entire class period (or day for elementary classes). These lessons should begin with an activity that will immediately engage the students and give the substitute a few brief minutes to get a feel for the class. An introductory activity that requires students to respond in writing to various questions (these can be written on the chalkboard or overhead projector) may look something like this:

> Write your name and date on a piece of paper and then answer these questions: What do you like best about this school? If you could have anything you wanted, what would you choose and why? (Note: I will be using this writing assignment to take attendance, so be sure your name is written legibly and that you turn in your work.)

Later in the class period or school day, this same assignment may be used to take roll, thereby saving time on managerial tasks while increasing instructional time. Substitutes may use any questions they like and should vary them often so that students are not presented with the same questions over and over again.

Generic lessons should be designed to provide learning activities for students that extend the regular curriculum in some way. Every state and school district uses a variety of tests to measure students' academic growth. Some of these tests emphasize writing skills, and all of them require that students be able to respond to various readings. Therefore, it makes sense to design generic lessons that substitutes can use that reflect those skills for which students are tested.

A very basic generic lesson would require students to read an article (preferably one related to the subject matter—science, art, sports, politics, local events, etc.), discuss the main ideas with a partner, and then share their views with the class while someone (the substitute or a selected student) records the responses on an overhead or chalkboard. This is a simple way of engaging students in both independent and group activities, and it easily transitions to whole-class discussions. This same activity can be expanded by having students write essays (e.g., summaries, analyses, rebuttals, editorials, etc.).

The key to any good generic lesson is that it reflects those skills that students are expected to learn, specifically in terms of critical thinking through reading, writing, discussing, and listening. Generic lessons can be written in advance (e.g., as a summer curriculum development workshop) for all subject areas in kindergarten through high school and kept on file at each campus. Whenever an emergency arises, the lessons are readily available.

Again, there is no foolproof way of ensuring that quality instruction will be taking place at all times in every classroom, but everything that can be done to help fulfill this expectation should be done. After all, every little bit helps. Providing user-friendly reference manuals with the necessary professional information, as well as useful, hands-on activities and suggestions, goes a long way toward making our goals more attainable.

User-Friendly Reference Manuals for Regular Teachers

Our regular teachers require the same consideration as our substitutes with regard to being prepared for an absence. It is best to keep the regular teacher reference manual simple. A manual that includes a rationale, focus, and objectives; suggestions for substitutes; guidelines for arranging substitute coverage; personnel information; and evaluation and feedback procedures can be organized into a three-hole-punched packet that regular teachers can keep in their roll books.

The rationale should be brief, yet contain the same emphasis on instruction as that written for the substitutes' manual. Regular teachers need to understand the importance of their preparation for an absence with regard to their professional responsibility to their students and their substitutes.

Ensuring that worthwhile instruction is taking place in the classroom at all times is the focus for any educator. Regular teachers need to be reminded that this includes those days during which they are absent and substitutes are teaching in their place. It sounds simple enough, but too often, instruction is the last thing that gets accomplished when the regular teacher is absent.

As with the substitutes' manual, the regular teachers' manual should also include objectives for the provision of such materials. One objective might state, "These materials are designed to help teachers prepare their students for substitutes."

The second section, suggestions for substitutes, should contain various kinds of information that have the potential of helping substitutes perform more effectively. There should be a place for the regular teacher to write out his or her schedule including room number(s), time of day (or periods), and subject(s) taught. It is very important that there also be a place for recording up-to-date seating charts for each class or period. Attendance forms or guidelines, passes, and lesson plans should also be included. There should be a place where the regular teacher can explain what he or she wants the substitute to do with his or her mail. Key personnel, such as the department chair or a colleague (name and location) who can assist the substitute, should be listed as well as the location of equipment (e.g., televisions, photocopy machines, tape recorders, etc.) and directions for how to check out such items.

A designated place for recording the names of reliable students for each class or period should be provided. Also, the regular teacher should leave clear directions as to where the substitute should leave any assignments that students turn in. Finally, included in this section may be some brief, generic lessons that any substitute could use in most classes.

One of the most important components of the regular teachers' manual is the section describing the guidelines that regular teachers are to follow for arranging substitute coverage. Many of the problems that substitutes face (e.g., short notice time, not knowing what they will be teaching, not arriving early enough to review the day's activities, etc.) can be eliminated simply by having the regular teachers carefully follow the procedure for arranging for coverage during their absence.

This section should be divided in half so that a thorough description of how to make arrangements for planned absences can be addressed as well as how to handle emergency situations. With regard to planned absences, most schools use standardized forms that regular teachers are expected to fill out and return to the principal's secretary at least 48 hours in advance. These forms ask for the teacher's name, social security number (for payroll purposes), date of the planned absence, subject(s) taught, class period(s), where materials for the substitute will be left, and if the immediate supervisor is aware of the anticipated absence.

There will also be a place to mark whether this absence is for school business or personal reasons. The form is usually approved by the principal before the secretary requests a substitute. Regular teachers are generally expected to call in prior to the end of the day on which they are absent to notify the principal's secretary of their return the following day or if they will need further substitute coverage. Failure to notify the principal's secretary can result in the regular teacher forfeiting substitute pay for those days.

In the case of unexpected absences, many large school districts have a substitute service whereby teachers call a specified number and leave a recorded message. Smaller districts often require teachers to call the principal's office. The information usually requested includes social security number, name, school, reason for absence (school business or personal reasons), subjects taught, time first class period begins, time last class period ends, and expected length of absence.

Aside from the basic procedures for securing a substitute, a section that explains various information specific to each campus should be provided. Cases in which there are any deviations from the general expectations should be clearly explained. This section should also include the names of all the principals, their schools, their telephone numbers, as well as the names and telephone numbers of their secretaries.

The final section of the regular teachers' manual should address evaluation and feedback procedures. The "Substitute Evaluation Form" and the "Substitute Feedback for the Regular Teacher Form" should be included for the regular teachers.

Reliable information goes a long way toward improving communication among administration, regular teachers, students, and substitutes. If people do not know what is expected of them, then they cannot be held accountable. However, when people know what they are supposed to be doing and have some guidelines for getting it done, then the expectation that it will be done is more than reasonable.

Summary

Perhaps the most important resource we can provide to substitutes is information. Reference manuals that are easy to use, detailed, and that address district, school, and classroom issues should be provided to all district substitutes. In addition, reference manuals for regular teachers can also help improve the effective management of substitutes.

The focus of these reference manuals should be on managerial responsibilities, district and school policies and practices, classroom management strategies, feedback and evaluation procedures, and generic lessons. Up-to-date information about the district and individual campuses as well as proper planning for absences will help ensure a smooth transition when substitutes replace regular teachers.

Staff Development

Growing to greatness as an educator is a never-ending process.

—Madeline Hunter

Staff development involves providing various interest groups with opportunities to increase their knowledge, develop and improve their skills, and expand their understanding of a given area of focus. The ultimate goal of any staff development program is to effect positive change in the classroom, specifically in interactions with students to promote learning.

Increasing the likelihood that a staff development program will be successful depends to some degree on the extent to which all stakeholders are included. With regard to the issue of substitute teaching, staff development workshops should be designed and implemented for principals and their secretaries, for regular teachers, and for substitutes. There should also be special sessions designed that include all of these groups and give them an opportunity to interact with one another.

Workshop for Principals and Their Secretaries

Principals and their secretaries are the individuals who are primarily responsible for managing substitutes at the campus level. Therefore, a 3-hour workshop can be designed to present general information regarding substitutes. This workshop should help principals refocus and refine their expectations of substitutes, examine their current programs, and update the materials and procedures that substitutes can use on their campuses.

Preparation for such a workshop should include the following:

Identify the Target Learners

The target learners for this workshop are principals and secretaries.

Determine the Target Setting

Principals and secretaries should implement skills learned at this workshop at their respective campuses.

Select the Topic for the Workshop

A suggested topic is "Making Your Campus User-Friendly for Substitute Teachers."

Acquire the Suggested Readings

Deay, A., & Bontempo, B. (1986). Helping substitute teachers contribute to school effectiveness. *The Clearing House, 59*(8), 359-362.

This article discusses the results of a study conducted to determine the kinds of information substitutes feel are of most value to them. The results focus on the perceptions of substitutes that it is the principal who is "the person who can create an atmosphere to enhance their effectiveness" (p. 362).

Drake, J. (1981). Making effective use of the substitute teacher: An administrative opportunity. *NASSP Bulletin, 65,* 74-80.

This article discusses the various problems that substitutes face and offers suggestions for addressing each. "The situation can be improved and the principal has the opportunity to make more effective use of the substitute teacher" (p. 79).

Esposito, F. (1975). Improving the role of substitute teachers. *NASSP Bulletin, 59,* 47-50.

As a former substitute teacher, Esposito suggests ways of improving the job that substitutes do. "The proper training and use of substitutes will cut down the untold thousands of wasted hours spent in American classrooms each year when regular teachers are absent" (p. 50).

Sendor, E. (1982). Use this test to spruce up your substitute teacher program. *The Executive Educator, 4*(6), 16-17.

This article provides a set of questions to help administrators assess the quality of their substitute teacher program—what is working and what areas could be improved.

Stanley, S. (1991). Substitute teachers can manage their classrooms effectively. *NASSP Bulletin, 75*(532), 84-88.

This article presents several classroom management skills and may be offered to substitutes as a form of inservice training. "Principals do not always have the time to prepare substitutes to manage their classrooms effectively and, therefore, ensure continuity of learning while the regular teacher is absent" (p. 84).

Gather the Needed Materials

1. Three-ring notebooks (one for each principal or campus)
2. Notebook dividers (one packet for each principal or campus)
3. Blank drawing paper and larger poster-sized paper
4. Crayons, markers, pens, and pencils
5. Substitute materials from the individual campuses and all district-provided substitute materials (principals and their secretaries should be asked to bring all substitute materials [e.g., manuals, check-in and -out forms, maps, bell schedules, etc.] used on their campuses to the workshop)

6. Overheads, handouts, and articles: workshop agenda, copies of articles (for each participant), "Campus Information for Substitutes" (see Resource B), and the workshop evaluation (see Resource C)

Write the Objectives

1. After examining and discussing their perceptions as to the effectiveness and shortcomings of their substitute teacher programs, and after reading the assigned articles, principals and their secretaries will be able to identify key information that should be provided to substitutes.

2. Using information from workshop discussions, handouts, articles, and overheads, principals and their secretaries will compile a substitute information notebook.

The workshop should be designed to include the following:

Present an Introductory Overview

1. Workshop participants will have 5 minutes to respond to these five questions regarding the realities and expectations of substitute coverage:
   a. Describe the procedures a substitute would follow if substituting on your campus. Start with the first thing a substitute would encounter upon arriving at your campus and conclude with what the substitute would do before leaving at the end of the school day. Also, list all materials and information distributed to substitutes on your campus.
   b. What are your expectations of substitutes while they are on your campus?
   c. What areas do you perceive to be strengths in how substitutes are "managed" on your campus?
   d. What areas do you perceive need to be changed or improved in how substitutes are "managed" on your campus?
   e. What do you hope to gain by attending this workshop on substitute teachers?
2. Participants will share responses to the introductory overhead. They will be asked to describe their perceptions of the substitute

coverage at their campuses and the expectations they have for improving their substitute teacher programs.

3. Using the overhead projector, the workshop trainer will list the expectations generated by the participants (e.g., classroom management skills, knowledge of broad range of subject matter, flexibility, punctuality, etc.).

4. Tell participants that the suggestions presented during the workshop for improving the effectiveness of their substitute teacher programs are starting points and that the value of any staff development program is in the ongoing implementation, evaluation, and revision of the program.

5. The objectives of the workshop should be shared with the participants (e.g., a handout or via an overhead projector). Give participants 3 or 4 minutes to read them.

Explain the Information That Will Be Covered

Lecture and discussion will be used to disseminate information to participants. Participants will work in groups of three and in pairs throughout the workshop when instructed to do so by the workshop trainer.

1. Participants will be given an overview of the information to be presented during the workshop.

2. Data on teacher absentee rates for each campus and the district as a whole, as well as surrounding school districts, will be presented. The presentation of these data on an overhead projector or handout may look something like this:

Schools	Number of Days Absent	× 5 Class Periods*
A	1,539	7,695
B	1,717	8,585
C	1,557	7,785
D	1,641	8,205
E	1,703	8,515
District Total:	8,157	40,785

*Note: The number of days absent was multiplied by five in order to show the approximate instruction time for which substitutes are responsible.

Surrounding School Districts

X	4,325 × 5 = 21,625 class periods per year
Y	11,091 × 5 = 55,455 class periods per year
Z	9,785 × 5 = 48,925 class periods per year

3. Participants will divide into groups of three (with at least one principal and one secretary from different schools in each group). Each group will discuss the importance of substitutes in providing coverage for absent teachers and the implications of the amount of time substitutes are delivering instruction. Discussion questions will focus on the following aspects:
   a. What are the implications for instructional continuity?
   b. What are the implications for academic achievement?
   c. What are the implications for a safe and orderly campus?
   d. What are the implications for efficient daily operations?
4. Each of the small groups will share its responses to the discussion questions with the whole group.
5. Participants will brainstorm what kinds of information they believe substitutes need to have in order to effectively carry out their responsibilities. Participants will work in their same groups of three.
6. Participants will read the five articles noted under the suggested readings section.
7. Participants will revise their list of information for substitutes, making any needed additions or deletions.
8. The workshop trainer will have each group write its list on a large sheet of paper and then post these sheets on the walls for all groups to see. The trainer will then have each group share its list. Participants will note those items that are repeated and compile a master list.
9. Items on the participants' master list will be compared with those items listed on the overhead "Campus Information for Substitutes."
10. Principals and their secretaries will then work together to answer the questions asked on the master list of items that substitutes need for their campus.

11. Participants will review and discuss guidelines for compiling substitute information notebooks. In determining what should be included, participants should refer to their earlier brainstorming, the articles reviewed, and the "Campus Information for Substitutes" overhead. The substitute reference manual should be divided into five categories: expectations and resource materials, campus procedures and general information, classroom materials, campus map and bell schedule(s), and evaluation procedures. At a minimum, participants should write outlines describing the information to be included in each section. Participants may also want to include handouts and forms already in use at their campuses, and some sections may be fully developed if time and resources permit.

12. Every principal and his or her secretary will compile a substitute information notebook for their school.

Review the Expected Feedback and Assessment

1. Participants will share their campus substitute plans with the entire group. Participants will offer comments and suggestions about each plan.

2. Participants will check each school's plan using the master list of needed items for substitutes to be sure that all areas have been addressed.

3. The workshop trainer will monitor group activity and keep participants on task by moving around the room, listening to discussions, answering questions, and providing minimal input.

4. Every principal and his or her secretary will compile a substitute information notebook for their school. A copy should also be sent to their supervisor for review and filing. This notebook should include such things as section dividers; campus map and bell schedule(s); explanations for various procedures (e.g., signing in, checking out, emergencies, nonteaching duties, etc.); expectations; evaluation procedures and forms; and related articles.

5. A staff development trainer will visit each campus to solicit feedback regarding the use of the substitute notebooks and will examine each book.

Plan the Workshop Wrap-Up

1. Give each participant a copy of the handout, *Workshop Evaluation*. Allow participants 10 min to respond.
2. Collect this handout.
3. Principals and their secretaries will take their substitute notebooks with them.

Workshops for Regular Teachers and Substitutes

Many school districts require their regular teachers to attend a half-day instructional inservice each semester. This is an ideal opportunity for offering regular teachers sessions related specifically to improving their substitute coverage.

The focus of these workshops should be on how to maximize instruction through better preparation. Questions that regular teachers should consider include the following:

1. What do I know about the substitute who will be filling in for me?
2. What kinds of activities can I leave for my students that will keep them actively involved in meaningful learning activities rather than mere busywork?
3. What do I need to tell my students about my absence and my expectations for their behavior?
4. Are my lesson plans easy to follow and complete? (Note: When students are required to complete their assignments and turn them in at the end of the period or school day, then they are more likely to feel that they are being held accountable for the work and will be motivated to stay on task.)
5. Have I left all the materials that the substitute will need in a location where they can easily be found?

Workshops for regular teachers can follow the same format as that described for the principals and their secretaries.

The most extensive staff development program should focus on substitutes, with intermittent sessions offered during the year:

Workshop	Length	Time
1st	7 hours	Prior to beginning of school year
2nd	2½ hours	During middle of first term
3rd	2½ hours	During middle of second term
4th	2½ hours	During middle of third term
5th	2½ hours	During middle of fourth term
6th	7 hours	During week following end of school year

The initial all-day workshop should be an orientation workshop. The substitute reference manual should be distributed at this workshop and provide the focus. A review handout can be designed to help participants get acquainted with the manual. Review questions should focus on the major sections of the manual and address key components within each section. The key to a successful workshop is to anticipate the needs of the participants and to remember that they are "adult learners."

In addition to this orientation workshop, follow-up workshops should focus on concerns that substitutes have and provide a forum for sharing their experiences, frustrations, and suggestions. Workshops that address specific topics can be designed according to the same format as that used with the principals and their secretaries. Topics may include "Substituting and Using Writing Across the Curriculum," "Tricks of the Trade—Favorite Stories, Games, and Activities for Elementary Children," and "What to Do With All That Energy—Keeping Middle School Students on Task."

The greatest potential benefit of offering quality staff development programs is in the area of student achievement. This goal can be accomplished both directly, through teachers' actions in their classrooms, and indirectly, by the benefits gained when teachers feel confident and enthusiastic about the environment in which they work. Successful staff development programs that provide all stakeholders with opportunities to participate help to build trust and understanding and promote clarity of focus, professional commitment, and an overall healthier school environment—especially with regard to our substitutes.

Summary

Professional growth opportunities for administrators and their assistants, regular teachers, and substitutes can be valuable in improving the use of substitutes and, in the long run, student achievement. Administrators need to improve their management of substitutes, regular teachers need to improve their planning for substitutes, and substitutes need to improve their instructional delivery.

Recommendations for Improvement

The purpose of schools is to transform children's lives every day.

—Lorraine Monroe

G iving substitutes every advantage and holding them account-able for their contributions may advance the understanding that substitutes are professionals and that they are an invaluable asset to the education system. The belief that it is unacceptable and not inevitable to lose valuable instructional time when a substitute is teaching may be projected through the development and implementation of the following recommendations.

1. Recruitment and selection practices for hiring substitutes may be improved by (a) encouraging a larger number of postbaccalaureate student teachers and interns to serve as substitutes; (b) advertising through the community newspapers and parent newsletters for substitutes; (c) publishing an overview of the district (its philosophy, goals, and programs); (d) following an interview process whereby the personal characteristics (e.g., a sense of humor, desire to work with kids, adaptability, etc.) and the professional attributes (e.g., content knowledge, previous teaching experience,

etc.) of prospective substitutes are assessed and a professional profile created; and (e) offering special consideration to those substitutes who desire permanent teaching positions when hiring within the district.

2. Professional development training could be offered specifically for substitutes in the areas of classroom management, technology, models of teaching, and content enrichment (e.g., interdisciplinary holistic writing, cooperative learning in foreign language classes, etc.). Prior to these specialized professional development offerings, all substitutes should be required to attend a 1-day inservice designed to provide substitutes with an overview of the district's policies and procedures as well as to present an ongoing forum for substitutes to share their experiences and explore alternative strategies for delivering effective instruction and managing students. A minimum of one follow-up inservice per semester should be designed for substitutes to allow ongoing opportunities for interaction with other professional educators and to receive any updated materials and information. Substitutes should be paid for this inservice time in the same way that teachers are paid for districtwide inservice days.

In addition to providing inservices for substitutes, principals, the campus person designated to handle substitute teacher assignments, and regular teachers should also receive inservicing on how to make effective use of substitutes. Training of principals and those individuals assigned to manage substitutes may help to ensure that substitutes are assigned to areas in which they can be most productive. Consequently, when principals are made aware of the roles that administrators, substitutes, regular teachers, and students can carry out, then each group can be held accountable and an increase in efficiency may be realized.

Teacher inservices designed to help regular teachers understand their professional responsibilities to their students and to their substitutes, and to provide them with strategies and models for preparing for substitutes when they are absent, may promote better lesson planning and preparation of students for substitutes; after all, regular teachers have the greatest influence in setting the tone for their substitutes. To increase the amount of instructional time, the time students are engaged—are "on task"—requires involving students in meaningful activities even on those days when a substitute teacher is teaching, and it is the responsibility of the regular teachers to leave lesson plans that reflect these outcomes.

It is critical that there be a smooth transition from the time substitutes are notified of their assignments through the carrying out of the lessons and finally, beyond the end-of-the-day checkout procedures. When all parties (administrators, regular teachers, students, and substitutes) understand their responsibilities, then substitutes will be able to perform their expected roles more effectively. To help ensure that these groups are informed and acting responsibly requires training, follow-up, and feedback; furthermore, it requires a financial commitment by the district to provide the necessary resources to offer professional development training.

A positive by-product of training substitutes is making clear the message that they are expected to be professional and deliver quality instruction. By providing a comprehensive substitute program, school districts may be able to attract better substitutes and, ultimately, better teacher applicants.

3. Evaluations of substitutes should be conducted on a routine basis by either the principal, an assistant principal, the appropriate supervisor, or a staff development specialist. A standardized form should be used uniformly for all substitute teacher evaluations. Areas of evaluation should include (a) personal characteristics (e.g., attitude, interactions with students, punctuality, etc.); (b) teaching characteristics (e.g., knowledge of content being taught, instructional delivery, ability to follow lesson plans, classroom management skills, etc.); (c) feedback left for the regular teacher by the substitute; and (d) managerial tasks completed (e.g., turning in daily attendance rosters). Evaluation of these areas can be assessed according to a quality scale with indicators such as "Outstanding," "Good," "Average," "Unsatisfactory," and "Not Observed." The evaluation form should also provide space for adding additional comments as well as a place for indicating whether the substitute teacher is recommended for continued reemployment at the campus. Finally, the evaluation form should include such identifying information as name of the substitute, date of the evaluation, class observed, length of the observation, and a place for the evaluator and substitute teacher to sign.

Additionally, substitutes should record their perceptions about their experiences. Helpful information includes dates of assignments, locations of assignments, content areas taught, names of teachers for whom they substituted, grade levels of students, lesson plans provided (it is recommended that substitutes keep a file of all lesson plans left by the regular teachers—either the original plans or photocopies), and a brief overview of those activities in which they participated (e.g., staff meetings, fire drills, assemblies, etc.). This kind of "professional log" is particularly beneficial for those substitutes pursuing permanent teaching positions. The recorded information can be shared with interviewers when substitutes apply for permanent teaching positions to show a history of their teaching experience as well as demonstrate their personal growth and conscientious professional attitude.

4. At least one person should meet with each substitute teacher after an evaluation to provide meaningful feedback for enhancing professional performance and for reinforcing those skills and qualities observed as strengths. Staff should make a special effort to thank substitutes and show their appreciation when a job is well done, and likewise, staff should address those incidents where a quality effort was not made.

5. Each campus should have a list of all substitutes in the district that identifies their name, area(s) of expertise, and number of years of teaching experience so that the person in charge of assigning substitutes to cover classes can be in the best possible position for matching substitutes with the content area(s) for which they are most qualified. A computer program could be designed to handle this kind of database information. Improving the use of substitutes at the campus level must be addressed from a managerial perspective (e.g., accurate and up-to-date lists) as well as from an innovative perspective (e.g., using campus staff as substitutes).

Administrators and all teachers on special assignments (e.g., Title 1 facilitators, staff development specialists, etc.) who are released from teaching full time should be required to substitute 1 day per month. The assignment of these individuals as substitutes should be a random process. The advantages of such a process include the following: (a) Money would be saved; (b) the number of days regular teachers are absent would possibly decrease because regular teachers would not know who their substitute might be; and (c) the quality of the lesson plans left for substitutes would most likely improve if regular teachers knew that an administrator, possibly even the principal, might be their substitute on any given day.

6. When substitutes are treated as professionals, they are more likely to be perceived as professionals; however, developing a positive professional perspective of substitutes will require a number of changes: (a) Quality substitutes will have to be hired; (b) ongoing professional development training will have to be provided; (c) routine evaluations of substitutes and evaluation postconferences will have to be conducted; (d) increased salary and benefits will have to be offered; (e) resources and support materials will have to be made available; and (f) substitutes will have to be professionally supported and valued by staff.

7. Instructional time is often wasted simply because there is no expectation that it can be productive; therefore, campus administration should be responsible for ensuring that all teachers have up-to-date seating charts and emergency lesson plans on file that involve students in interactive lessons, as opposed to mere "seat work" assignments. Additionally, periodic checks of the kinds of lesson plans left for substitutes should be conducted. The kinds of materials left for substitutes should integrate managerial tasks with instruction, thereby maximizing the amount of time students are engaged in worthwhile learning activities. Learning activities should provide opportunities for individual, small group, and whole-class learning through active participation, and they should focus on critical thinking through reading, writing, discussing, and listening. In using such instructional devices, some or most of the class time often lost when a substitute teaches may be regained.

8. All pertinent information that will improve the effectiveness of substitutes should be made available to them prior to their assignments. For example, substitutes should receive information packets regarding district policies and procedures prior to the beginning of the school year. A reference manual for substitutes should be provided that addresses the following five areas: an overview of the general expectations and conduct policies of the

district; specific information regarding the central office and the individual campuses; various feedback and evaluation forms that substitutes are expected to use as well as the evaluation form that will be used in assessing substitute performance; suggestions and strategies for substitutes to use in dealing with students; and lessons and helpful hints for how to be prepared at all times for all occasions.

Upon arriving for an assignment at the campus, every substitute should be given information that will enable him or her to successfully carry out his or her expected tasks. First, substitutes need a map of the campus, keys, and accurate bell schedules. Second, the items essential for substitutes to manage classes effectively are up-to-date seating charts and thoroughly explained lesson plans. Finally, feedback and support from staff, students, and administration may enhance the overall performance of substitutes.

9. Substitute teachers must act quickly and be ready at a moment's notice to fulfill any number of teaching assignments. To optimize the skills and resources of substitutes, early notification is imperative. The ideal situation for all parties involved is to call substitutes the night before they are needed. This allows substitutes time to prepare mentally and physically for the rigorous demands awaiting them the following day.

10. Offering fringe benefits, such as health care coverage and accident insurance, may attract a larger pool of substitutes from which to choose. Increasing the daily rate of pay for substitutes may also contribute to finding and retaining quality substitutes and may increase the likelihood that there will be enough substitutes to cover classes during times of high demand.

Having an adequate supply of substitutes is important, but reducing the number of substitutes needed at any given time must also be examined. To reduce the number of days that substitutes are needed, school districts could also increase the retirement "buy-back" amount for unused personal days of regular teachers from 30% to 50% of the regular teacher's unused days. Another incentive to reduce the number of substitutes used by regular teachers is to give each teacher an additional $300 at the beginning of the school year. For the first six times a substitute is hired for that teacher, the substitute's salary (based on the current $50 per day) would be paid for out of this $300 stipend. Any additional substitute days would be paid for out of the district substitute fund following the normal procedure. Any portion of the $300 remaining at the end of the school year would belong to the regular teacher.

11. An inexpensive change in the practices of using substitutes would be to hire a designated number of permanent substitutes for each campus based on the number of regular teachers assigned to that campus. For example, a large campus whose teaching staff averages between 150 and 300, would maintain a pool of 10 substitutes. These substitutes could be given any number of incentives, including long-term substitute teaching contracts, higher pay (e.g., $65 per day rather than $50), health care benefits, and special consideration if they desired permanent teaching positions at that campus or elsewhere within the district. On days when all substitutes in this pool were not needed to teach, they could be assigned various tasks, including working in administrative offices, tutoring students, or aiding regular teachers.

By adding substitutes to the intricate operations of a school, they would have opportunities to learn the names of administrators, staff, and students. In addition, they would have firsthand knowledge of the operations of the campus—the day-to-day activities that are observable as well as those that are merely implied and perceived only through personal experience. Understanding the larger scope of a school is just as important as adapting to its many individual class environments. Using permanent substitutes may promote better communication and stronger professional attachments between substitutes and schools.

Addressing the problems surrounding the effective use of substitutes requires awareness of the need, a sense of responsibility to our students, and commitment to making real changes. For too long we have relied on short-term, crisis-driven interventions for managing our substitute teacher programs; as a result, we are shortchanging our students. Education is a demanding process that depends on continuity, focus, and relevancy. We can no longer afford to throw away valuable instructional time. We must maximize our opportunities to provide quality instruction to all students at all times.

Summary

There are many ideas that can be implemented to improve substitute programs. Considering the prolonged lack of attention given to this issue, real change will require a major overhaul, beginning with recruitment and hiring procedures and extending through to managing and evaluation practices of substitutes.

For too long, nothing has been done; the situation has been ignored in the foolish hope that everything will work out. Unfortunately, it is our students who have paid the price. We must work together to maximize instruction every day, in all classes, for every student. The time has come to take action—there is so much we can do simply by paying attention and wanting to make things different. This is a beginning.

Resources

Resource A

FEEDBACK FOR THE REGULAR TEACHER

Date: _____

_____ for _____
Substitute's Name   Regular Teacher's Name

Directions: Attach additional pages to this form as needed.

1. Did you receive lesson plans? ____ Yes____ No
2. Please describe (or attach) the lesson plans left for you.
3. How did you implement the lesson plans and what did you accomplish?
4. Was the time allotted for instructional activities adequate?
5. Did you encounter any problems? Please describe.
6. In general, please describe the students' behavior.
7. Were you effective? Did you do a good job? How do you know?
8. How could you have done a better job?
9. In general, how would you describe this teaching experience?

10. Please note any deviations from the lesson plans.
11. Did you give any new assignments? Explain.
12. What positive feedback can the regular teacher give to his or her students?

NOTE: This form is to be completed prior to checking out *each* day and left for the regular teacher.

Resource B

CAMPUS INFORMATION FOR SUBSTITUTES

(It may be helpful to give this list to principals and their secretaries prior to the workshop.)

Name of School
School Address and Phone Number
Contact Person
Location of Contact Person
Procedure for Reporting In and Checking Out
Bell Schedule(s) and Campus Map (staff bathrooms highlighted)
Parking for Substitutes
Keys for Substitutes (where to get them)
Location of Lesson Plans and Seating Charts
Emergency Procedures and Contact Person
Whom to Contact as a Last Resort for Disciplinary Action
Lunch Procedures
Expectations of Substitutes
Campus Administrators and Responsibilities
Procedures for Assigning Grades and Completing Student Reports
Procedures for Contacting Parents
School Calendar
Procedures for Evaluation
Nonteaching Duties
Legal Issues and Professional Conduct
Fire Drill Procedures and Evacuation Map

Resource C

WORKSHOP EVALUATION

Directions: Please use the following scale to best describe how you feel about each statement (5 = *agree strongly;* 4 = *agree;* 3 = *neither agree nor disagree;* 2 = *disagree;* 1 = *disagree strongly*):

1. This workshop has helped me better understand the needs of substitute teachers.

   5   4   3   2   1

2. This workshop has helped me better understand the importance of giving substitute teachers information about my campus.

   5   4   3   2   1

3. I believe substitute teachers are important professionals and should be treated as such.

   5   4   3   2   1

4. I believe substitute teachers *do* play an important role in the education process.

   5   4   3   2   1

5. I believe substitute teachers make an important contribution to student achievement.

   5   4   3   2   1

6. I believe that providing substitute teachers with helpful and relevant information about my campus will help them be more effective.

   5   4   3   2   1

7. What was the *most* useful part of this workshop?
8. What was the *least* useful part of this workshop?
9. How could this workshop be improved?
10. What additional information would you like about substitutes?
11. What are your recommendations for improving the effectiveness of substitutes in this district?

Annotated Bibliography and References

Benedict, K. C. (1987). Student expectations and the substitute teacher. *The Clearing House, 61,* 27-28.

This article emphasizes the perceptions of students and offers a questionnaire designed to determine student expectations. The intent is to encourage students to take responsibility when a substitute teaches and to see another point of view.

Bontempo, B. T., & Deay, A. M. (1986). Substitute teachers: An analysis of problem situations. *Contemporary Education, 57*(2), 85-89.

This article focuses on a study regarding the various problems and needs of substitutes and helps clarify that substitutes understand their responsibility to do more than just baby-sit.

Chu, L., & Bergsma, H. (1987). How principals can help substitutes. *Principal, 67*(1), 44-45.

This article offers specific guidelines to help principals successfully design inservice for substitutes.

Clifton, R. A., & Rambaran, R. (1987). Substitute teaching: Survival in a marginal situation. *Urban Education, 22*(3), 310-327.

This article focuses on a study about the difficulties substitutes have because they have no real authority and they lack an un-

derstanding of classroom routines. It is administrators and regular teachers who must help substitutes be a part of the professional staff.

Dilanian, S. M. (1986). *Dimensions of needs in secondary substitute teaching.* Michigan. (ERIC Document Reproduction Service No. ED 277 686)
This study provides a brief review of research and literature about substituting and offers suggestions for helping substitutes to be more effective.

Drury, W. R. (1988). Eight ways to make sure substitute teachers aren't baby-sitters. *American School Board Journal, 175*(3), 51.
This article offers specific ideas for revamping substitute teacher programs.

Freedman, M. K. (1975). The new substitutes: Free to teach. *NASSP Bulletin, 59*, 95-98.
This article focuses on basic statistics regarding substitutes, including the number of days taught and salaries. Suggestions are offered for improving perceptions, maximizing class time, and identifying the roles of administrators, regular teachers, students, and substitutes.

George, P. L. (1984). How to improve your substitute teaching program. *Tips for Principals.*
This article presents questions administrators can use to assess their substitute programs, how to screen potential substitutes, and what to do to make improvements.

Johnson, J. M., Holcombe, M., & Vance, K. (1988). Apprehensions of substitute teachers. *The Clearing House, 62*(2), 89-91.
This article reports on a study related to the role of substitutes, specifically with regard to their apprehensions and what regular teachers and administrators can do to improve the situation.

Koelling, C. H. (1983). Substitute teachers: School policies and procedures in the North Central Region. *Education, 104*(2), 155-171.
This article reports on a study that examined the policies and procedures pertaining to the success of school districts in achieving good substitute teacher programs.

Kraft, D. W. (1980). New approaches to the substitute teacher problem. *NASSP Bulletin, 64*(437), 79-86.

This article presents recommendations for improving substitute programs, including what principals can do, how to implement orientation sessions, and what feedback procedures can be used.

Meara, H. (1983). *Class coverage in the Chicago public schools: A study of teacher absences and substitute coverage.* Chicago: Chicago Panel on Public School Policy and Finance.

This study of substitute coverage in the Chicago public schools focuses on the financial aspects of teacher absences. This is a study of the policies and practices that govern the administration of teachers' absences, number of absences, and substitute coverage. It identifies problems with the substitute program and offers recommendations for improvement.

Rundall, R. A. (1981). Give your sub a break. *The Clearing House, 55*(1), 43-44.

This article focuses on what regular teachers, department chairs, and administrators can do to improve the effectiveness of substitutes.

St. Michel, T. (1994, May). *Substitute teachers: Who? What? How? When? Where? Why? A case study of the substitute process.* Unpublished doctoral dissertation, Arizona State University, Tempe.

This comprehensive study of the substitute teacher program in the Phoenix Union High School District (a large urban school district) focuses on (a) accurately describing substitutes—their roles and expectations, professional and personal experiences and backgrounds, and working conditions; and (b) offering recommendations for improving the hiring, training, evaluating, and retaining practices of substitutes.

Tracy, S. J. (1988). Improve substitute teaching with staff development. *NASSP Bulletin, 72*(508), 85-88.

This article offers suggestions for engaging substitutes in ongoing staff development focusing on orientation programs, classroom management and instructional techniques, skills reinforcement, and increasing lines of communication and resources.